BUTTERFLY
PA KUA CHANG
(EIGHT TRIGRAMS PALM MANEUVERS)

BY

AL CASE

(THE MASTER FOUNDER)

AL CASE

QUALITY PRESS

For information regarding this material go to:

MonsterMartialArts.com

ISBN-13: 978-1511981804

ISBN-10: 1511981806

Copyright © 2004 by Alton H. Case

All rights reserved. No part of this material may be reproduced or transmitted in any form or by any means, electronic or mechanical, including photocopying, recording, or by any information storage and retrieval system, without the written permission of the author.

That is why it is called the Form of the Formless,
The image of Nothingness.
That is why it is called the Elusive;
Meet it and you do not see its face;
Follow it and you do not see its back.

The Tao

BUTTERFLY PA KUA CHANG

TABLE OF CONTENTS

	SPECIAL NOTE FRONT HE AUTHOR	4
	MY PURPOSE IN THE MARTIAL ARTS	5
	INTRODUCTION	7
1	THE PA KUA SYMBOL	9
2	A SHORT HISTORY	10
3	HOW TO MAKE A CIRCLE	11
4	HOW TO WALK THE CIRCLE	12
5	WALKING THE CIRCLE	14
6	LOW/LOW	22
7	THE TEN HANDS	24
8	LOW/MIDDLE	26
9	TEN HAND FUNCTIONS	28
10	LOW/HIGH	30
11	STRIKING	32
12	LOW/CIRCLE	33
13	BODY INTEGRITY	35
14	MID/MID	36
15	HARMONY	38
16	MID/HIGH	39
17	FORCE AND FLOW	41
18	MID/CIRCLE	42
19	THROWING	44
20	HIGH/HIGH	45
21	THE SIZE OF THE CIRCLE	47
22	HIGH/CIRCLE	48
23	CREATING WORLDS	51
24	CIRCLE/CIRCLE	52

EIGHT ANIMALS PA KUA CHANG

	INTRODUCTION TO THE SECOND SECTION	54
25	THE BUTTERFLY	55
26	HARD VS SOFT	62
27	THE CRANE	64
28	THE FLOW CHART	71
29	THE SNAKE	73
30	AIKIDO	81
31	THE MONKEY	82
32	TRUSTING THE CONCEPT	89
33	THE DRAGON	90
34	ANALYSIS OF ART	95
35	THE LION	96
36	THE USE OF FORCE AND FLOW	103
37	THE PHOENIX	105
38	2BCBM	112
39	THE TIGER	113
40	LOVE YOUR FELLOW MAN	119
41	CREATING PA KUA CHANG	121
	EPILOGUE	124
	ABOUT THE AUTHOR	125

AL CASE

A Special Note from the Author

This is the original manuscript from the original Butterfly Pa Kua Chang course. The only changes, aside from a few typos, have been to reformat the book to fit this version.

This book originally came with an accompanying video. Search on Amazon for this, or look to my website, MonsterMartialArts.com

MY PURPOSE IN THE MARTIAL ARTS

I want to say something here. I want to discuss what my true purpose is here.

I am not out to destroy arts, or grind any particular political ax. Quite the contrary, I want to improve the martial arts. I want to upgrade the martial arts on this planet.

The only way to do this is to introduce the concept of physics, to actually teach people, instead of having them monkey see-monkey do for a lifetime.

What good is something, no matter how many times you do it, if you don't understand it?

What this means is that you have arrived at the front door. You have the opportunity to delve into the martial arts, to understand them as never before, and to share that understanding with the entire planet.

Once you understand Matrixing, you become the supreme instructor, and the entire planet is your classroom.

No matter where you go, should you choose to talk, others will listen.

I'm telling you right now, when I start talking about matrixing, people shut up and drop their jaws. The truth is so simple that people actually slap their heads when they first hear it.

And you can be the one that knows, that the audience listens to, and for one simple reason: you know what you are talking about.

No more, 'My Master can beat your master,' and 'My art has been taught monkey see-monkey do for twenty generations and nobody really knows what it is about anymore but it sure is impressive, isn't it?"

Instead, simple workability.

And I am telling you, plain and simple, people will shut up and listen when you say, 'The reason this technique works is because....'

And then they get it, and they blink at the sudden enlightenment, and they become the teachers for a planet that is sadly lacking in the common sense of physics.

And they are forever grateful to you for being the first person on this planet, in their lives, no matter how many schools they've been to, and no matter how systems they know, who actually teaches them something. **WHO MAKES THEM UNDERSTAND!**

INTRODUCTION

Pa Kua Chang, an art that immediately offers the concept of mysticism and superhuman powers.

Well, it should. It should because of all the martial arts, it is the one that came closest to matrixing.

Oh, there are hints of matrixing in every art, but usually those are drill specific, and not aimed at aligning entire arts.

Pa Kua Chang was different.

Pa Kua Chang had eight animals, and these eight animals were matrixed, creating every single combination of animals, and thus defining an entire art.

Where it fell short was that it didn't have matrixed drills, and it didn't matrix all the arts.

But for what it did, for how far it went, it was, is, pretty spectacular.

Unfortunately, in just the short time since its inception, it has undergone profound change that eats away at the matrixing concept inherent within it.

Everybody has a favorite theory, or something they think is more important and should be concentrated upon, and the definition of animals becomes complex, and moves Pa Kua towards the unattainable.

Not good.

The purpose of this course is to redefine the animals in their simplicity, to matrix, again, the initial concepts of the art.

Further, to aid in this process, and to further define matrixing, and thus to safeguard, as much as possible, against erosion, the beginning of the course concerns itself with the Ten Arms.

The Ten Arms defines the energy bearing constructs of the body. To not know those, or to go against those, frustrates the entire art.

This all being said, one question deserves answer: how long does it take to master.

Well, the originator is said to have walked the circle for near a dozen years.

It must be observed, however, and with respect, like most inventors, he had only a vague idea of where he was going.

Using the method in this course should shorten the time to results to a year or two.

When I first studied this art I gathered every bit of material I could, and walked the circle for an hour or two each day.

I kept my knees to ninety degrees. I sweated 'silver' water. Quite amazing, that, but it told me that I was heading in the correct direction.

After two years, I experienced actual 'lightening' shooting up and down my legs when I maneuvered. Further, where I had walked the circle was so impacted that the ground was harder than concrete.

Okay, enough talk. It's your turn.

Do it.

CHAPTER ONE
THE PA KUA SYMBOL

THIS IS THE OFFICIAL PA KUA CHANG SYMBOL. OBVIOUSLY EXTENSIVE THEORY HAS GROWN AROUND THIS SYMBOL.

AT THE HEART OF THE SYMBOL IS THE YIN YANG. IT IS SURROUNDED BY EIGHT TRIGRAMS, WHICH CAN BE STUDIED TO UNDERSTAND ALL THE PERMUTATIONS OF LIFE.

CHAPTER TWO
A SHORT HISTORY

A little over a hundred and fifty years ago there was a man named Tung Hai Chuan. Little is known about Tung Hai Chuan, but it can be surmised that he studied the martial arts, and he eventually came into contact with a certain religious sect in China which believes in walking in a circle and chanting mantras. Tung combined walking the circle with the martial arts, and so was born Pa Kua Chang.

Tung is supposed to have disguised himself as a eunuch and gone to work in the Imperial palace. There, he supposedly was noticed by the Emperor himself because of his sure footedness in crowds, and eventually have undergone a challenge by the Imperial bodyguards. The end result is that he was called upon to share his art, and did.

How much of this is fact and how much is rumor this author doesn't know. Tung is also purported to be able to disappear from his student's sight, speak from beyond the grave, and so on.

Myth, legend, rumor, fact, it is up to you to decide, draw upon whichever to inspire yourself, for this is an art to be inspired in.

Pa Kua Chang translates as 'Eight Palm Maneuvers.' It is known as a very serpentine art, wriggling and writhing, smooth and flowing, wily and wise.

It has also become renowned as a very serious study of self-defense.

Furthermore, and this is of high interest, students of Pa Kua tend to have speed, strength, calmness, patience, in short, all the attributes of the most excellent martial artists.

Lastly, people who study Pa Kua tend to have excellent health and long lives.

CHAPTER THREE
HOW TO MAKE A CIRCLE

PA KUA CHANG IS THE ART OF WALKING THE CIRCLE.

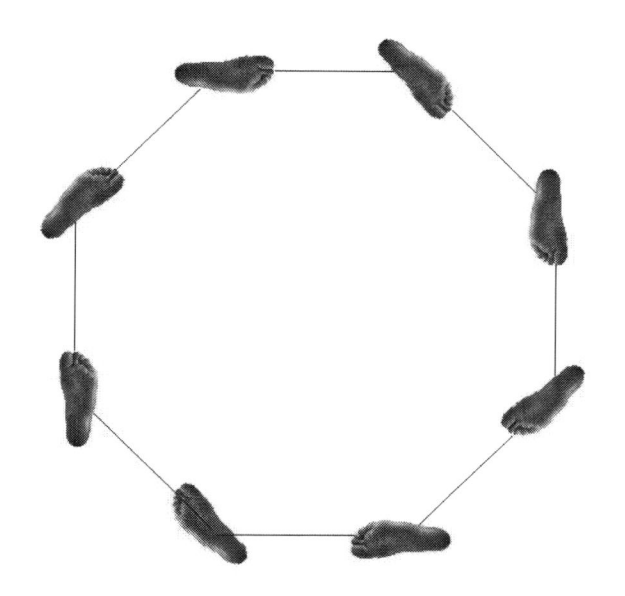

DRAW A CIRCLE ON THE GROUND, IT SHOULD BE LARGE ENOUGH THAT YOU CAN TAKE EIGHT SHOULDER LENGTH STEPS.

CHAPTER FOUR
HOW TO WALK THE CIRCLE

There are several books concerning Pa Kua Chang, and Walking the Circle has been described adequately. So this description will be brief and succinct, so as not to waste your time. Let me just say, before I describe the technical circle, that Walking the Circle is the most important part of Pa Kua Chang. I trust this will become clearer through your perusal of this book. At any rate, learning to relax and create the World of the Circle is worth ten thousand techniques. Indeed, it, the Circle, is the birthplace of Infinite Technique, should you be intelligent enough to settle for the simplicities. So...

1) I recommend studying a 'hard' art before Pa Kua Chang, as basic Martial Arts principles should be understood before attempting this advanced study. Also, many people are not strong enough (especially in the energetical sense) to effectively walk the circle without first strengthening their body (again, energetically) through a hard art.

2) The circle should be about 6 feet across, and should have eight points (an octagonal shape) to place your feet upon.

3) When placing your feet upon the circle point them at the next spot on the circle, unless you are preparing for change of direction.

4) First, roll your feet when walking, as if each sole is a rocking chair. Feel the weight moving through the foot at an even rate of speed. Beginners wobble in the shoulders, then the hips, then the knees, then the ankles, and at last the

wobbling will stop. This means that their awareness has reached the ground, and they may begin the next type of walking. It is not important to go low at this stage, but it certainly doesn't hurt.

5) Make sure, when you are walking, that the body moves at an even rate of speed around the circle. The head should not lurch forward and back like a giraffe's, the hips should not go up and down or forward and back, and the idea is to move the Tan Tien at an even rate of speed, with no body part lurching to throw it off.

6) The next stage of walking is called flat walking (Mud Walking). Place the foot down so that the whole sole touches as one. Make sure the body floats at an even rate of speed, as described in number five.

7) Go slowly, especially at first. The success of Circle Walking is to become aware of the circle, and of the way your body works within the circle. Concentrate on keeping the lumbar bones in the small of the back stacked, and the hips tucked forward. Get lower as you are able.

8) If Walking the Circle alone concentrate upon your finger, or hand, depending upon what you are doing. If Walking the Circle with a partner concentrate upon keeping eye contact and letting the world pass by. In this manner you create a unique world, beyond the real world, where the art of Pa Kua will exist and become real and more than sufficient to handle the attacks of the real world.

CHAPTER FIVE
WALKING THE CIRCLE

Stand in a natural position. the feet should be shoulder width apart. The balance should be so that you can move in any of the eight directions of the compass easily.

Circle the left through a cross palm and scoop the right under the left elbow. You should be shifting towards the right.

Continue circling the left across the body as you raise the right in a spiraling motion. More weight shift to the right.

Settle the weight on the right in a back stance as you lower the right hand in the guard position (Butterfly block) and protect the body with the left.

Take a step on the circle. The hand should be as if placed upon a pole placed in the center of the circle, and the eyes should watch the fingertips. Letting reality slide past your fingers enables you to create your own Pa Kua universe.

Take another step on the circle. You should concentrate on the weight, as if was an actual ball, going up and down your legs. This pulsing up and down creates an alternating energy to and from the Tan Tien (the one point, the center of your body which is located an inch or two below your navel). Thus, the tan tien becomes a generator which will create a unique energy.

Take another step on the circle. Make sure you breath in time with the pulsing of energy.

Take another step on the circle. You should be bending your knees to ninety degrees (though this make take some practice), and moving very slowly.

Take another step. Concentrate on your unbendable arm. Imagine yourself inside a bubble.

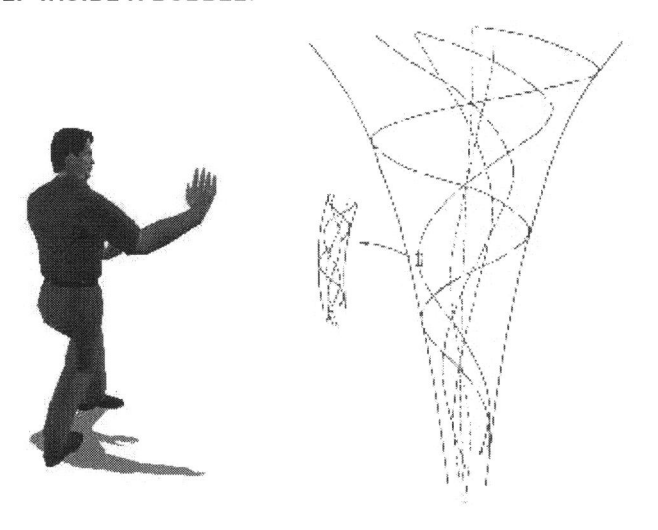

Take another step. Note that there is a twining motion in the limbs. This will create a spiraling type of energy within. This spiraling is actually a vortex of energy which, if you do it long enough, becomes so efficient that it creates a vacuum in the center of the limbs, which center, being hollow, will suction energy through the limb.

Take another step. note how closely the knees brush. Note how the feet are always pointed towards the next spot on the circle. The hips should move through space at an even, unchanging rate of speed.

Take another step. you are at the beginning of the circle, and it is time to change direction.

Pivot. If you are confused, examine the data on Pa Kua walking in the Diagram Boxing section of this website.

Note how you travel through the cross palm block and then spiral your other hand upwards.

Settle into a stance and walk the circle in the other direction.

CHAPTER SIX
LOW/LOW

BOTH ARMS ARE IN THE LOW POSITION. VISUALIZE YOURSELF AS HAVING THE HAND INSIDE THE CIRCLE UPON A GIANT SCREW, AND ONLY BY WALKING AROUND THAT SCREW, PUTTING THE WHOLE BODY WEIGHT THROUGH THAT SCREW, CAN YOU SCREW IT TO THE GROUND. MAKE SURE THAT YOU LOWER YOURSELF AS THE SCREW GETS LOWER.

LOW/LOW APPLICATION

The attacker kicks to the groin with the right foot.

The Defender cross steps forward and to the left with his right leg while hooking the Attacker's leg with the right arm of the Low/Low.

The Defender walks the circle into the Attacker while lifting the leg.

CHAPTER SEVEN
THE TEN HANDS

While traditional Pa Kua practitioners deal in eight specific hand positions, I deal in ten specific arm positions. These are:

Low/Low
Low/Middle
Low/High
Low/Circle
Middle/Middle
Middle/High
Middle/Circle
High/High
High/Circle
Circle/Circle

These arm positions cover virtually every arm position the arm makes. How the arm is used will define the hand configuration. So I don't define the arm usage by the hand configuration, but rather hand configuration by the direction the arm takes to do the job. There are only six specific directions one need concern oneself with in this analysis. These are:

RIGHT
LEFT
UP
DOWN
BACKWARDS
FORWARDS

Sometimes the arm direction and the hand configuration won't mesh, so you choose a different combination of the hand configuration and arm direction.

CHAPTER EIGHT
LOW/MIDDLE

THE HAND INSIDE THE CIRCLE TURNS THE SCREW IN THE LOW POSITION. THE HAND OUTSIDE THE CIRCLE CARRIES A WAITER'S TRAY SHOULDER HIGH. RAISE THE PINKIE AND LOWER THE THUMB TO CREATE SPIRAL TENSION THROUGH THE ARM.

LOW/MIDDLE APPLICATION

THE ATTACKER PUNCHES TO THE BODY WITH HIS LEFT HAND.

THE DEFENDER CROSS STEPS FORWARD AND TO THE LEFT WITH HIS RIGHT LEG AND HOOKS UNDER THE ATTACKER'S ARM WITH THE RIGHT OF THE LOW/MIDDLE.

THE DEFENDER WALKS THE CIRCLE INTO THE OPPONENT, KEEPING THE ATTACKER'S ARM TRAPPED, SNAKING THE LEFT ARM UNDER THE ATTACKER'S ARM AND ACROSS HIS CHEST WHILE TURNING HIS WAIST TO THE LEFT.

CHAPTER NINE
TEN HANDS FUNCTIONS

There are eight sides to the circle, and the Pa Kua student should be able to execute blocks in eight directions from those eight sides. The multiplicity of combinations off this simply stated concept is virtually endless.

Yet, in reality, the function of Pa Kua is simple. There are only so many things one can do.

The True Beginning is in walking laterally around the sphere of your opponent, no matter the attack. This is why simply walking the circle is so incredibly important to the realization of the Pa Kua art.

The actual function of Pa Kua is based upon the fact that there are only four potentials that one must be aware of. The opponent must reach you with either one of two hands, or one of two feet. Each of these two hands and two feet can be blocked (maneuvered) from one of two sides. What this means is that One Circle in two directions simplifies the possibility of four attacks. This means that there are only eight potentials for entering your sphere.

CIRCLE COUNTERCLOCKWISE ON:
RIGHT KICK
LEFT KICK
RIGHT HAND
LEFT HAND

OR CIRCLE COUNTERCLOCKWISE ON:
RIGHT KICK
LEFT KICK
RIGHT HAND
LEFT HAND

At this point, however, we are not concerned with the eight entering zones, however, beyond listing them. What is more important is to list the obvious functions of the ten hands.

I should say, right now, that when I speak of the ten hands, I am invariably referring to the ten arm positions, which are the combinations of the four basic arm positions.

The ten arm positions are:

Low/Low	Sweeping the kick up
Low/Mid	Lower splitting
Low/High	Upper armlock
Low/Circle	Elbow bracing
Mid/Mid	Upper splitting
Mid/High	Inserting
Mid/Circle	Arm rolling
High/High	Inserting
High/Circle	Crossing Under
Circle/Circle	Harmonizing

Please know that while I have listed specific functions, other functions are possible, and in individual cases, may be preferable. Exercise yourself in this concept, but do not allow yourself to be swayed, or to teach, other than the ten arm positions.

CHAPTER TEN
LOW/HIGH

THE ARM INSIDE THE CIRCLE TURNS THE SCREW. THE HAND OUTSIDE THE CIRCLE PUSHES FORWARD AND UPWARD, THE HAND IN FRONT OF THE FACE, THE PINKIE TURNED DOWN AND THE THUMB TURNED UP TO CREATE SPIRAL ENERGY.

BUTTERFLY PA KUA CHANG

LOW/HIGH APPLICATIONS

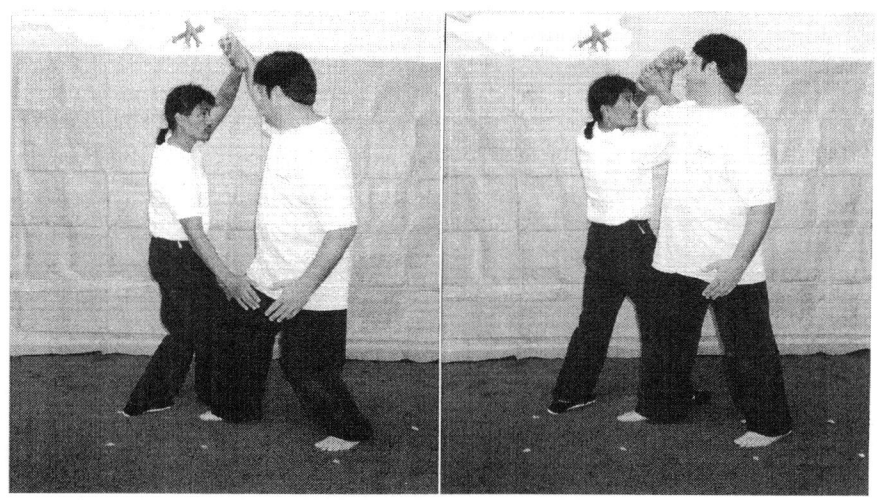

THE ATTACKER PUNCHES TO THE BODY WITH HIS RIGHT HAND.

THE DEFENDER CROSS STEPS FORWARD AND TO THE LEFT WITH HIS RIGHT LEG. SIMULTANEOUSLY, HE PUSHES THE ATTACKER'S RIGHT ARM UP AND BACK WITH HIS LEFT HIGH ARM AND SLAPS THE ATTACKER'S GROIN WITH HIS RIGHT HAND.

TAKING ANOTHER STEP IN THE CIRCLE THE DEFENDER SNAKES HIS RIGHT HAND UNDER THE ATTACKER'S RIGHT ARM AND EXECUTES AN UPPER ARMLOCK.

CHAPTER ELEVEN
STRIKING

There is a fifth arm position, which is thrusting or striking. However, to strike in a thrusting manner destroys the continuity of the circle, also, the extended arm becomes a lever available to one's opponent. So in Pa Kua striking is usually done in a 'By the way,' manner with the arm still circled. This means the circling won't be broken or disrupted, and the integrity of the body as one unit can more easily be maintained.

CHAPTER TWELVE
LOW/CIRCLE

THE HAND INSIDE THE CIRCLE TURNS THE SCREW. THE HAND OUTSIDE THE CIRCLE CURVES AROUND SO THAT THE HAND IS IN A KNIFE EDGE POSITION IN FRONT OF THE BODY MOVING FORWARD ON THE LINE OF THE CIRCLE.

LOW/CIRCLE APPLICATION

The Attacker punches to the body with the right hand.

The Defender steps forward and to the left with his right leg while executing a parry with his right Low arm and assuming a left circle position with his left arm.

Taking another step in the circle and pivoting into the Attacker, the Defender circles his right hand up to the Attacker's forehead and executes a left elbow strike to the back of the Attacker's neck.

CHAPTER THIRTEEN
BODY INTEGRITY

Body integrity means using the body as one unit. This means not falling to the use of muscle, because to use muscle isolates body parts and destroys the ability of the body to flow energy in one continuous stream.

This is actually a form of CBM. CBM mean Coordinated Body Motion, and is when all parts of the body support one intention.

Utilizing CBM the body becomes 'unbendable.' This is like the unbendable arm of Aikido, except that it is the whole body that becomes unbendable, and one utilizes the circle Walking of Pa Kua to move this unbendable unit through space.

CHAPTER FOURTEEN
MID/MID

BOTH ARMS ARE CARRYING 'WAITER'S TRAYS' SHOULDER HIGH. PINKIES UP AND THUMBS DOWN FOR SPIRALING ENERGY.

MID/MID APPLICATION

THE ATTACKER PUNCHES TO THE FACE WITH THE RIGHT HAND.

THE DEFENDER STEPS FORWARD AND TO THE LEFT WITH HIS RIGHT FOOT WHILE BLOCKING THE ATTACKER'S ARM WITH HIS ARM IN THE RIGHT MIDDLE POSITION AND HOLDING HIS LEFT ARM IN THE MIDDLE POSITION.

THE DEFENDER TAKES ANOTHER STEP IN THE CIRCLE, PLACING HIS LEFT LEG BEHIND THE ATTACKER'S LEG AND SNAKING HIS LEFT ARM ACROSS THE NECK OF THE ATTACKER TO 'SPLIT' THE ATTACKER'S HEAD AND BODY.

CHAPTER FIFTEEN
HARMONY

Body Integrity harmonizes energy of the body throughout the body.

CBM harmonizes the motions of the body through space.

Two Body CBM (2BCBM) harmonizes the opponent's body.

Think of it this way: when your body is perfectly in synch and running smooth, the bodies around it want to be that way also. So by avoiding those moves which go against another person's body, Two Body CBM may be achieved, and you can literally take control of another persons body without him realizing it, or being able to do anything about it.

Being able to do this is real Third Level Martial Arts.

CHAPTER TWELVE
MID/HIGH

The hand inside the circle is forearm level, palm vertical and away from the body, the forefinger bones stacked, and the other fingers slightly clawed.

The hand outside the circle pushes forward and upward with the same hand configuration, but the index finger pointing into the middle of the circle.

MID/HIGH APPLICATION

THE ATTACKER STRIKES TO THE FACE WITH THE RIGHT HAND.

THE DEFENDER CROSS STEPS FORWARD AND TO THE LEFT WITH HIS RIGHT LEG. THE RIGHT ARM (MID) HOOKS OVER THE ATTACKER'S ARM.

THE DEFENDER CONTINUES WALKING THE CIRCLE INTO THE ATTACKER AND SNAKES HIS ARM AROUND THE ATTACKER'S HEAD TO EFFECTIVELY 'ENCIRCLE' THE ATTACKER.

CHAPTER SEVENTEEN
FORCE AND FLOW

The Force and Flow Formula states:

> If the Force is greater Flow it,
> if the Flow is greater Force it.

In circling we are usually flowing. But what if we decide, for whatever strategic or ethical reason, to deal in Force? This means that we will forsake the lateral movement and go directly towards the opponent, utilizing full Body Integrity and CBM to deliver the full weight of the body, magnified by whatever velocity we can achieve.

CHAPTER EIGHTEEN
MID/CIRCLE

THE HAND INSIDE THE CIRCLE IS FOREARM LEVEL, FOREFINGER BONES STACKED, PALM AWAY, THE OTHER FINGERS SLIGHTLY CLAWED.

THE HAND OUTSIDE THE CIRCLE IS IN THE SAME HAND CONFIGURATION, BUT ON A LINE BETWEEN THE TAN TIEN AND THE INSIDE HAND, POINTING TOWARDS THE INSIDE HAND. THIS ENABLES IT TO PROTECT THE 'DOOR' UNDER THE INNER ARM. THIS IS THE CLASSIC 'READY' POSITION OF PA KUA CHANG.

MID/CIRCLE APPLICATION

The Attacker punches to the face with the right hand.

The Defender cross steps forward and to the left with the right leg. With the right Mid he blocks the Attacker's arm inward.

Taking a quick step around his own leg and back into the Attacker, the Defender pulls the Attacker's arm down with his right hand while pushing up on the elbow with his left hand to achieve an Elbow Roll.

CHAPTER NINETEEN
THROWING

The basic idea in throwing is to utilize your opponent's arm, legs or head (or the spine directly) as levers to contort his spine until he he is unable to stand. There are two major concepts in this act.

Rotary Throwing is the circling of the limbs until the opponent crashes.

Insertion Throwing is inserting a body part into your opponent's structure. Insertion may be a throw by itself, but many times it only leads to Rotary Throwing.

CHAPTER TWENTY
HIGH/HIGH

THE ARMS ARE RAISED FORWARD AND UPWARD IN FRONT OF THE BODY IN THE DIRECTION OF THE CIRCLE. TILT THE PINKIES BACK AND THE THUMBS FORWARD TO INCREASE SPIRAL ENERGY.

HIGH/HIGH APPLICATION

The Attacker punches to the face with the right hand.

The Defender cross steps forward and to the left with his right leg while raising his arms to the inside of the Attacker's arm.

The Defender inserts his right arm next to the Attacker's neck and pushes on the arm while pulling on the neck. He continues his circling while doing this and the Attacker spirals into the ground.

CHAPTER TWENTY-ONE
THE SIZE OF THE CIRCLE

The size of the circle depends upon the depth of penetration. There are four specific depths.

Circling the wrist
Circling the Elbow
Circling the Should
Circling the axis

You may circle either direction on any of these four joints which, interestingly, gives one eight potentials.

Incidentally, if you push the Attacker's limb across his body it is called 'closing.' If you push the Attacker's limb away from his body it is called 'opening.' Closing is better, but both closing and opening lead to various, precise series of follow up circles.

CHAPTER TWENTY-TWO
HIGH/CIRCLE

THE HAND INSIDE THE CIRCLE IS IN FRONT OF THE BODY, UNDER THE OUTER HAND, KNIFE EDGE IN THE DIRECTION OF THE CIRCLE. THE ELBOW ANGLES INTO THE CIRCLE. THE HAND OUTSIDE THE CIRCLE PUSHES FORWARD AND UPWARD.

HIGH/CIRCLE APPLICATION

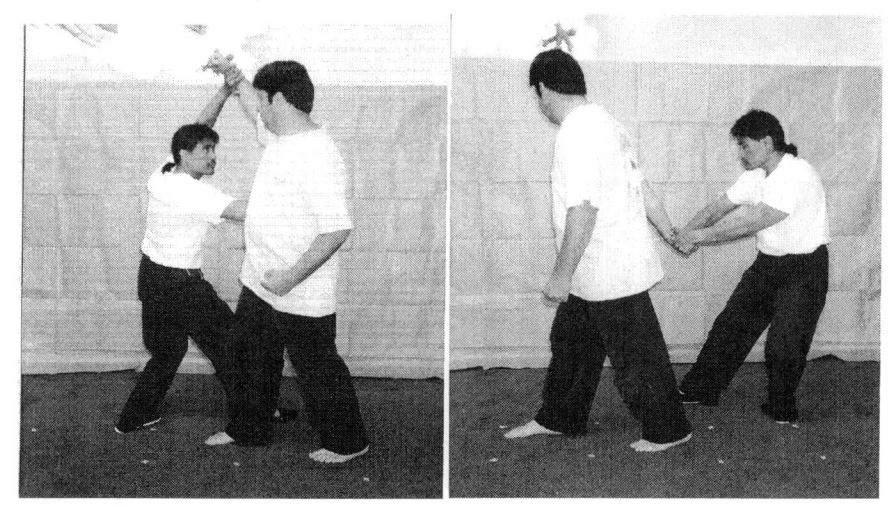

THE ATTACKER PUNCHES TO THE HEAD WITH HIS RIGHT HAND.

THE DEFENDER CROSS STEPS FORWARD AND TO THE LEFT WITH HIS RIGHT FOOT. PUSHING UP ON THE ATTACKER'S LEFT HIGH ARM HE EXECUTES A RIGHT ELBOW TO THE RIBCAGE.

THE DEFENDER CONTINUES THE MOTION OF THE ELBOW STRIKE, STEPS UNDER THE BRIDGE OF THE ATTACKER'S ARM AND PIVOTS HIS BODY WHILE HE RETAINS A GRIP ON THE ATTACKER'S RIGHT WRIST WITH HIS LEFT HAND.

Stepping backwards with his left foot he executes an armbar.

CHAPTER TWENTY-THREE
CREATING WORLDS

The secret to effective Pa Kua is the ability to create a world separate from the so-called 'real world.' Here are some advices to help you do this.

1) When walking the circle alone watch your raised index finger so that your attention is locked on it and the real world slides by.

2) When walking the circle with a partner look at each other so that the real world slides by.

3) While walking the circle you may come to feel like you are floating (while not relinquishing your ability to ground, but, rather, enhancing it). This is good. At this point you will understand what 'Stillness in Motion' is.

4) True Pa Kua will not manifest until you are able to trust your opponent. This means to trust him to do exactly what he is going to do (because you know what he is going to do because you have practiced for so long.)

CHAPTER TWENTY-FOUR
CIRCLE/CIRCLE

THE ARMS ARE IN FRONT OF THE BODY, KNIFE EDGE FORWARD IN THE DIRECTION OF THE CIRCLE

CIRCLE/CIRCLE APPLICATIONS

The Attacker punches to the face with the right hand.

The Defender steps forward and to the right with his right leg while catching the Attacker's arm.

Once the Defender has harmonized his opponent he may choose a direction in which to throw or otherwise manipulate him.

EIGHT ANIMALS
PA KUA CHANG
INTRODUCTION TO THE SECOND SECTION

Having finished the first section, you should be able to walk the circle and hold 'unbendable' arms as you do so. This means that anybody who attacks you will be misdirected as they slide off your arms and angles and changes.

At worst, they will be crunched by your mere motion, and you should be able to push people off their stance merely by bracing against them, lowering yourself, and walking.

There is more.

Now, to be truthful, all the tricks of exploding or pulsing energy are in other courses, and, to be honest, being able to hit somebody is not the essence of Pa Kua; being able to avoid...and guide and misdirect and confuse and bamboozle others is what Pa Kua is about.

If you have to strike somebody in Pa Kua, then your Pa Kua has already failed.

Practice harder.

Having said that, let me say that the following section, which deals with the 'Eight Animals' of Pa Kua, is going to help you in this matter.

Yes, there will be strikes, and that aplenty.

However, the most important theory is going to be dealing with body motion.

Lots of this stuff is covered on the video, however, lots of it isn't.

Some of it, as simple as it is when written down, is hard to talk about, or to describe sufficiently using just body motion.

I know that sounds odd, but that has been the weakness, and the strength, of true Pa Kua.

CHAPTER TWENTY-FIVE
THE BUTTERFLY

Good Pa Kua has a flow, yet it is unpredictable in its changes.

The forms you see in this section are classical, though I have altered names according to my own purposes.

Stand in a natural position. the feet should be shoulder width apart. The balance should be so that you can move in any of the eight directions of the compass easily.

Turn the left foot and the hips to the left. The arms should move away from the body and the body should be moving as

ONE UNIT. THE LINE OF THE RIGHT FOOT SHOULD BE NINETY DEGREES TOT HE LEFT OF THE LINE OF THE RIGHT FOOT.

STEP TO THE LEFT WITH THE RIGHT FOOT TO THE FIRST CORNER OF THE CIRCLE. THE LEFT ARM CIRCLES TO A PALM POSITION, THE RIGHT ARM IS SCOOPING UNDER THE LEFT ELBOW. THE FEET SHOULD BE POINTED INWARD.

CONTINUE PIVOTING THE BODY TO THE LEFT. THE RIGHT ARM STARTS TO 'SWOOP' UPWARD.

PIVOT TO THE RIGHT WITH THE HIPS, THE RIGHT FOOT AND THE RIGHT HAND. THE WEIGHT OF THE BODY IS SHIFTING OVER TO THE LEFT FOOT.

THE LEFT FOOT MOVES PAST THE RIGHT FOOT. THE BODY CONTINUES TO PIVOT AS ONE UNIT TOWARDS THE CENTER OF THE CIRCLE.

SIDE VIEW OF LAST PICTURE.

CONTINUE STEPPING WITH THE LEFT FOOT TO THE NEXT CORNER OF THE CIRCLE. THE RIGHT ARM TURNS OVER SO THAT THE ARM IS 'UNBENDABLE,' AND THE PALM IS UPRIGHT (BUTTERFLY POSITION) WITH THE PALM BONE PRESENTED. THE TIPS OF THE FINGERS SHOULD BE LEVEL WITH THE EYES.

WALK THE CIRCLE TO THE ORIGINAL POSITION, DO THIS FORM IN REVERSE, AND WALK BACK TO THE BEGINNING FOR THE CHANGE INTO THE CRANE.

BUTTERFLY APPLICATION

The Attacker prepares to punch.

The Attacker steps forward with the right foot as he executes a right punch. The Defender steps forward and to the left with the left foot as he executes a Butterfly block.

The Attacker steps forward with the left foot as he executes a left punch. The Defender steps forward with the left foot, the right hand slips the punch.

The Attacker executes a right punch. The Defender takes a step to the right with the right foot as he executes a left Butterfly block.

Look, people, I could give you endless applications, and you could memorize them, but there is something more important here: a concept.

The concept is that the Attacker attacks, and you place a Butterfly block up to absorb the attack (or slip him with the back hand). But you are not blocking (although that may occur), you are letting him bounce off your 'Unbendable arm.'

So the concept is this, the Attacker attacks, and the Defender walks, and no matter what the distance or effort by the Attacker, the Defender must keep the Unbendable arm in place by utilizing his footwork.

The Feet Control the Distance!

Once the Attacker can be negated whenever he steps forward with the same side punch, then you can move into attacks where he steps forward with one foot and attacks with the opposite arm.

Then you can mix them.

And then you can fend off (control) multiple strikes, and so on.

Remember, you can destroy an attacker at any time, but that is not The True Art. The True Art is in controlling your attacker.

CHAPTER TWENTY SIX
HARD VERSUS SOFT

When I teach Pa Kua I usually teach two applications for each animal.

I will teach an easy, obvious strike, such as a simple butterfly block, and then I will teach an easy, obvious grab art.

I then tell students that they must matrix everything.

First, and easiest, is the matrixing of the hard. They simply set up (ask their partner) for the strike that will fit the block they are doing.

I don't worry about footwork too much on the hard matrix. If they hold a face to face position, or move when striking, I don't much care.

Next I have them matrix soft to the hard.

For instance, I will have them strike, then apply a grab art from each animal.

Butterfly/butterfly

butterfly crane

butterfly snake

and so on.

While this is sometimes difficult, and poses interesting problems, it can still be handled by asking for appropriate strikes.

However, there is a curve of randomness here.

Can you apply a particular animal no matter what the attack is?

Which is to say, whether the partner strikes high or low, can you apply the animal easily?

This does tend to get interesting.

Finally, third step, I ask the student to matrix the soft applications.

This is where the student starts to think, and where Pa Kua really starts to bite.

The student is encouraged to move, move, move, and he must adapt to any strike, no matter what trajectory the strike may have, with a particular animal.

To sum it up:
First level--matrix hard to hard.
Second level--matrix hard to soft.
Third level--matrix soft to soft.

Man, when you reach the third level, you are really on the way!

CHAPTER TWENTY-SEVEN
THE CRANE

The first thing you should do is learn that you are bigger than your opponent; you can encircle him. Practice this move with much grace and flow. Practice it slowly, with attention to detail, and eventually you will be able to move your whole body faster than your opponent can move a fist.

Stand in a natural position. The feet should be shoulder width apart. The balance should be so that you can move in any of the eight directions of the compass easily.

Shift your weight to the right foot as you extend the left arm and raise the right arm as you pivot to the left. The left foot should pivot so it is facing 90 degrees from the lines of the right foot.

Step to the left with the right foot as your left arm is extended in a low block and the right arm is raised in a high block. The weight shifts to the right.

Pivot the body to the right as you shift your weight to the left foot. The right arm swoops down and the left arm swoops up to execute a crane posture to the right.

Begin stepping around the right foot with the left foot as you begin bringing the right arm up and the left arm down.

Place the left foot on the next spot on the circle as your arms assume the on guard position.

Walk the circle and do the form on the other side.
Then walk the circle back to do the next form.

CRANE APPLICATION

The Attacker prepares to punch.

The Attacker steps forward with the right foot as he executes a right punch. The Defender steps forward and to the left with the left foot as he executes a Butterfly block.

The Attacker executes a left strike. The Defender cross steps in front of the Attacker with the left foot as he brings the left arm over and down. The right arm is raised up for encirclement.

The Defender takes a step with the right foot, walking the circle around the Attacker. The left arm comes up to entrap the Attacker's left arm, and the right arm circles behind the Attacker's neck.

BUTTERFLY PA KUA CHANG

The Defender steps behind his right leg with his left leg. His encirclement is working, and he guides the Attacker's arm and head. At this point the Defender should be more concerned with the purity of the circle, letting it be pure, virtually ignoring the Attacker, makes it work better. This is because intention will start to flow.

The Defender twists his body to the left (in the direction he was stepping.) The Attacker's arm is broken, and his neck and spine are at risk.

Now you can keep twisting, completing breaks and making throws, but a fun thing to do, at this point, is to change directions, pivot in the other direction. It may seem awkward at first, but with practice you will find a whole bunch of fun things to do with the Attacker's body.

This is a great second technique, as it translates an attack into a grab art with the greatest of ease. You will find that the concept of matrixing is going to be applied through this art. You may want to take a look at Matrix Karate so that you will fully understand this concept.

Incidentally, the technique works even better if the idiot is coming at you with a kick.

CHAPTER TWENTY-EIGHT
FLOW CHART

On the following page you are going to see something called a flow chart.

Perhaps you have heard my tale, of how I wished to 'solve' the martial arts as a puzzle, and how, after some thirty years, I sat down and made thousands of little cards listing all the techniques I knew, and how I eventually whittled these down to the 'workables.'

A very slim number when compared to the total.

Well, that's where the story starts. What I did then was make a flow chart, and I found out where each and every technique actually fits.

And here is something interesting.

You can check techniques which are 'just' karate, and they will describe a certain geometry on the flow chart.

And you can do the same for every single art.

Yes, there is the problem of some arts 'borrowing' from other arts, and thus becoming untrue.

However, if you can force yourself to subscribe to the 'geometric theory' described by analysis of the flow chart, you can understand each art in a separate and pure manner that has never been known before.

Not only does the geometry define technique, but it illuminates core concepts behind arts in such a way that they become instantly usable.

Holy fanatic, Batman, this is the secret of the True Art!

So, take a look at The Flow Chart, see if it makes sense, and we will examine further, later, after you have done so.

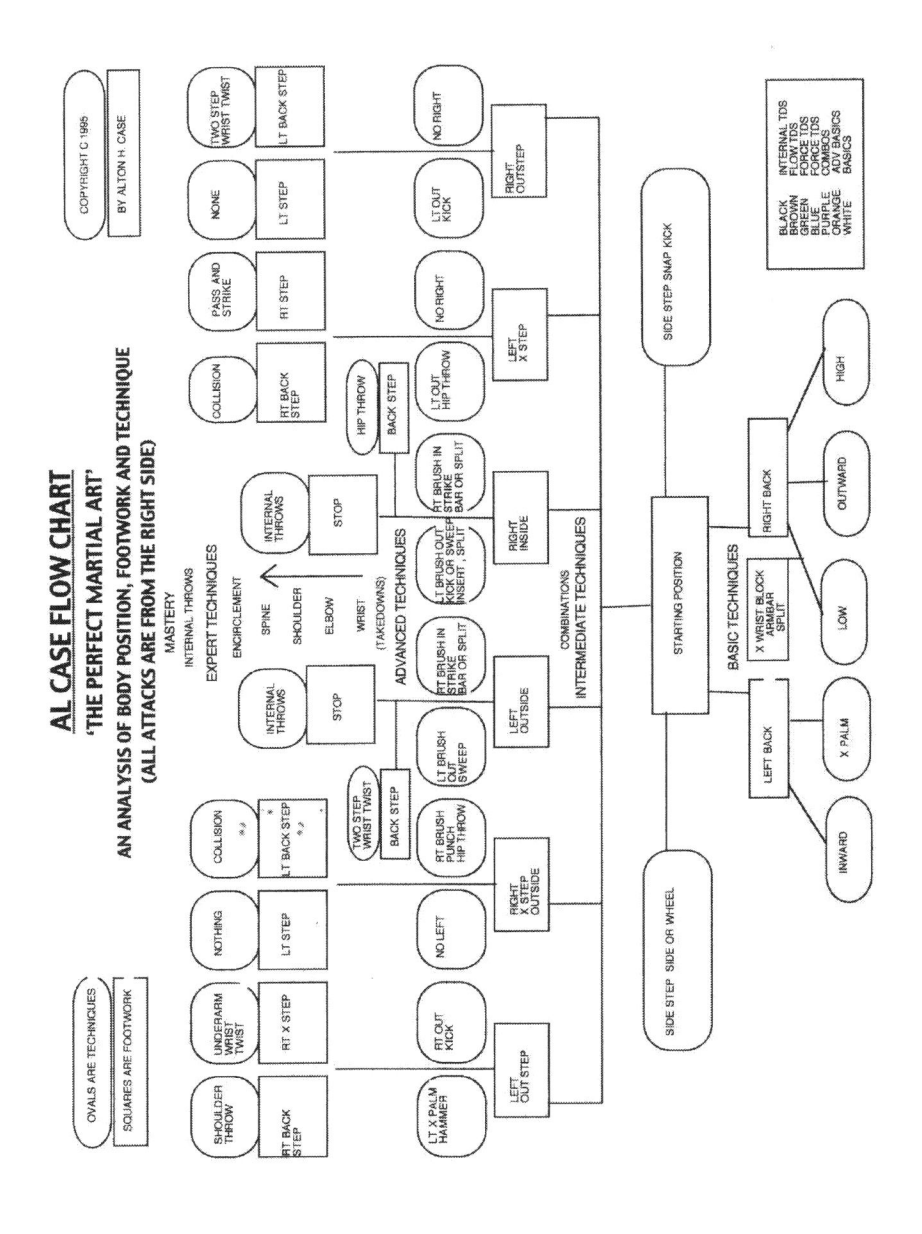

AL CASE FLOW CHART
"THE PERFECT MARTIAL ART"
AN ANALYSIS OF BODY POSITION, FOOTWORK AND TECHNIQUE
(ALL ATTACKS ARE FROM THE RIGHT SIDE)

CHAPTER TWENTY-NINE
THE SNAKE

Make sure the energy of the snake flows out of the tan tien. (The Tan Tien is the energy center of the body, it is located approximately two inches below the navel.)

Stand in a natural position. the feet should be shoulder width apart. The balance should be so that you can move in any of the eight directions of the compass easily.

Extend the left arm and raise the right arm as you pivot to the left.

Step to the right with the right foot as your left arm is extended in a low block and the right arm is raised in a high block. This is the crane position.

Pivot to the right, the left hand circles around into a palm block. The right hand swoops downward (palm turned earthward).

Continue pivoting to the right, the weight shifting to the left leg. The left hand parries, and the right comes upward with the fingers INSIDE the left arm as you execute a left parry and right (palm upward) spearhand.

Step forward with the left foot, turn the right hand outward as you move the body as one movement.

Walk the circle and do the form on the other side. Then walk the circle back to do the next form.

BUTTERFLY PA KUA CHANG

SNAKE APPLICATION

The Attacker prepares to punch.

The Attacker steps forward with the right foot as he executes a right punch. The Defender steps back with the left foot into a back stance as he executes a left parry and begins a right spear hand uppercut.

In pivoting to the left the Defender pulls the Attacker's arm out enough so that he may insert his right spear hand under the Attacker's right arm at about the elbow.

The Defender pivots to the right as he pulls the Attacker's arm up at the elbow and down at the wrist. The Defender's left hand is a little high in this picture, so you can better see it. You will have to figure out the correct angles for different size bodies, anyway.

The Defender steps back with right foot as he pivots to the right and begins to throw the Attacker. Examine how the right hand works and figure out how to get it to the other side of the Attacker's arm. If you do it wrong you'll slap yourself in the face with his hand.

Finish the pivot as you snake your left hand over the elbow. Also, you might be able to find a wrist lock with your right hand. You can throw the Attacker, or you can lock him onto the ground.

While this difficult looks difficult in the beginning, you'll find it is quite easy with just a little practice.

While I have shown the technique with a step backwards by the Defender, it can be done by stepping into the Attacker, which would more closely approximate the concept of circle walking around the Attacker.

Also, once learned, this technique should be done matrix style with the rest of the Pa Kua techniques.

Chapter Thirty
Aikido

I used to teach a seminar called 'Instant Aikido.'

I claimed that I could get somebody to do Aikido within a couple of hours.

Oh, the complaints.

You can't do that!

And, it was usually traditionalists that made the largest fuss.

Well. I understand that. They have invested thousands of hours into something esoteric and incomprehensible, and I claim to make it usable and comprehensible in a couple of hours. No wonder they felt a little, shall we say...shortchanged?

Now, I was able to do this, I am going to tell you the secret right here, by simply telling the student to circle his arms, so that he circled his opponent's joint (and it didn't matter which joint) until he found a jointlock.

I augmented this by telling the fellow to do one of two footworks.

A simple two step, which is the essence of Aikido footwork, or to cross step, which is the beginning of Walking the Circle.

And there it was.

Aikido.

Oh, it was raw, unpolished, but workable.

And with a simple list of jointlocks, and maybe ten hours of seminar, I could probably make these fellows look like they had twenty years experience.

I am not kidding.

What, you think I am kidding?

Well, e-mail Mike@MonsterMartialArts.com and ask him if he plans to produce the video tape I made of the whole thing!

Heh heh!

CHAPTER THIRTY-ONE
THE MONKEY

This posture has a variety of names: White ape offers fruit. Monkey offers peach, etc. I just call it the monkey.

Stand in a natural position. the feet should be shoulder width apart. The balance should be so that you can move in any of the eight directions of the compass easily.

Pivot to the left. The weight will shift onto the right leg and the arms make circle at shoulder level with the palms facing out.

Step to the left with the right foot and pivot until you are facing left. The circle of your arms should expand, as if they are opening a pair of sliding doors. Your weight should be on the right leg.

Pivot to the right, Going through an hourglass stance the arms circle out and down as if you are about to scoop something up.

Continue pivoting to the right and bring the hands up as if offering up a small plate.

Step around the right foot with the left foot to the next position on the circle. The left arm slides down (without really touching) the right arm, and the right arm swings out towards the ready position.

Walk the circle and do the form on the other side. Then walk the circle back to do the next form.

Remember to walk slowly and feel the energy (weight) going up and down the legs.

One of the things you can do is keep the arms in the dragon 'spread out' position and walk the circle with them extended. Break posture only when you are turning into the next position.

MONKEY APPLICATION

The Attacker prepares to punch.

The Attacker steps forward with the right foot as he executes a right punch. The Defender steps slightly forward and to the left with the left foot as he executes a Monkey posture to trap the Attacker's arm.

To be honest, there are probably a hundred different techniques that could be executed now. And, to be specific, in my arts one would probably use this technique as an entry technique to Monkey Boxing. (See the 'Monkey Trap' technique in Matrix Kung Fu.) Following is a technique more specific to

Pa Kua, and which will enable you to better see the relationship of walking the circle to application of form. Please note that the technique is more 'go with the flow,' Aikido style, etc. Can you find the alternative to this one, which is to step to the right, then step with the left behind your right (this is a spinning movement across the Attacker's body)? It will take a higher degree of timing to make it work.

The Defender steps back and behind himself with the right foot. This sets up a spinning motion which, because the Attacker is firmly lodged in the Monkey technique, will cause him to awkwardly follow along.

Now, reverse your direction (step back the way you came with the right foot) and close line the sucker. Leave a card recommending a doctor on his sleeping chest and hightail it out of there.

CHAPTER THIRTY-TWO
TRUSTING THE CONCEPT

If you examine the Flow Chart you will see that Pa Kua involves moving towards and to the side of the opponent with a cross step.

The cross step is the start of the circle.

And, if you happen to 'accidentally' step with the wrong foot, then you are starting the Two step, which is the essence of Aikido.

Now, you could merely move the arms in circles, but you should evolve some plan which will put the arms into one of the 'unbendable' positions.

And you should breath from the tan tien (a point some two inches below the navel which happens to be the energy generator for the body).

This rather simple process, of stepping in a certain direction and manner, while moving (holding) the arms just so, and generating mucho energy, is what the whole thing is all about.

Now, to make it all work, consider that your opponent will either attack, or flee.

He will move towards you, or away from you.

If he moves towards you, adjust so that the distance is controlled by you, and then choose to shade towards him, or away from him, in a manner that will benefit some technique.

I tell you, it really is that simple.

When I first started doing this stuff I was a big faker.

I would just do what I have just told you, and then let whatever technique happened to develop develop.

I tell you, I did not have a plan, just a concept, and the concept never failed me, so I became something more than a faker.

I always trust the concept more than the technique.

CHAPTER THIRTY-THREE
THE DRAGON

Spread the energy out and walk as one unit.

Stand in a natural position. The feet should be shoulder width apart. The balance should be so that you can move in any of the eight directions of the compass easily.

Pivot to the left. The weight will shift onto the right leg and the arms extend slightly to the sides.

Step to the left with the right foot and pivot until you are facing left. Your arms should circle out and over until they are in a cross parry to the left. Your weight should be on the right leg.

Pivot to the right, the weight shifting to the left leg, as you fold the hands in and extend them to the sides (double outward blocks with the palms up.)

Step around the right foot with the left foot to the next position on the circle. The right arm should start turning over and the left arm should start crossing the body.

Walk the circle and do the form on the other side.
Then walk the circle back to do the next form.

Remember to walk slowly and feel the energy (weight) going up and down the legs.

DRAGON APPLICATION

The Attacker prepares to punch.

The Attacker steps forward with the right foot as he executes a right punch. The Defender steps slightly forward with the right foot as he executes a double parry over the Attacker's wrist.

The Defender steps forward and behind the Attacker's right leg as he parries the Attacker's punch to the right and traps it with his right arm, and extends his left arm across the Attacker's chest. The Defender's knee should close with the Attacker's knee, breaking his connection to the ground and further aiding the technique.

This is a wonderful technique which illustrates how the circle should be used to direct an aggressive defense.

Interestingly enough, this, and all Pa Kua techniques, can be done so as to either open or close an Attacker.

CHAPTER THIRTY-FOUR
ANALYSIS OF ART

There are actually several stages within the martial arts, and the arts take on a specific form of development.

TAE KWON DO	FIXED POSITION	FORCE
KARATE	FIXED POSITION	FORCE
KUNG FU	FIXED POSITION	FORCE/FLOW
PA KUA CHANG	UNFIXED POSITION	FLOW
TAI CHI CHUAN	FIXED POSITION	FLOW

The above examples are, unfortunately, tainted by not being pure in concept. With the courses offered at Monster Martial Arts these arts can describe the geometries and conceptualizations described, and can become pure.

You should make lists of other arts, and understand them on conceptual levels.

Furthermore, and this is a doozy, you should create a matrix of fixed and unfixed positions and matrix it with force and flow, and see if there is a specific art that has never been developed.

Since arts 'borrow' from one another so freely (in an attempt to cope, instead of evolving to come to grips with alien and unknown attacks) there will be much confusion. But as you continually distill and resolve arts, they should become more pure.

CHAPTER THIRTY-FIVE
THE LION

This is sometimes called 'Lion rolls the ball.' Pa Kua names usually tend to be flowery, and I am sure there was an original intent to express the motion and the flow of power with a poetic flare, but sometimes the imagery seems forced. This one is more like scoop up a bag and toss it over the shoulder.

Stand in a natural position. The feet should be shoulder width apart. The balance should be so that you can move in any of the eight directions of the compass easily.

PIVOT TO THE LEFT, THE WEIGHT GOING ONTO THE RIGHT LEG. THE ARMS SWING SLIGHTLY OUT TOT HE SIDES.

STEP TO THE LEFT WITH THE RIGHT FOOT, THE WEIGHT GOING TO THE RIGHT FOOT AS YOU SCOOP THE HANDS UPWARDS.

PIVOT TO THE RIGHT AS YOU BRING THE HANDS UP AND THE SEPARATE THEM SO THAT THE RIGHT EXECUTES A RIGHT BUTTERFLY BLOCK AND THE LEFT EXECUTES A HIGH BLOCK.

Step around the right foot with the left foot as you bring the arms into the butterfly position.
Walk the circle and do the form on the other side.
Then walk the circle back to do the next form.

BUTTERFLY PA KUA CHANG

LION APPLICATION

THE ATTACKER PREPARES TO PUNCH.

THE ATTACKER STEPS FORWARD WITH THE LEFT FOOT AS HE PUNCHES WITH THE LEFT HAND. THE DEFENDER STEPS BACK WITH THE RIGHT FOOT INTO A BACK STANCE AS HE EXECUTES A LEFT BUTTERFLY BLOCK.

The Attacker executes a right punch. The Defender steps forward with the right foot as he passes the Attack with the left palm. Footwork is based upon a triangle here.)

The Attacker finishes his punch as the Defender steps back with the left leg into a back stance and executes a right butterfly palm.

BUTTERFLY PA KUA CHANG

The Defender steps forward with the left foot, he is starting to walk the circle as he raises the left hand to encircle the Attacker.

Circling all the way in the Defender encircles the Attacker's neck.

The Defender spins, thus circling the Attacker around.

The Defender reverse direction, thus clotheslining the Attacker.

CHAPTER THIRTY-SIX
THE USE OF FORCE AND FLOW

A fight is won by controlling distance; by letting all the action happen at the distance(s) that most benefit you.

A fight that is conducted with force is already lost.

Somebody is going to get hurt.

So, in the interests of saving my fellow man from force and violence, let me offer the following concept.

There are two possibilities: the opponent goes towards you, or away from you. (He will not be capable of the true creative offered by slanting to the side because he is the attacker.

An attacker, by virtue of being an attacker, must come towards you.

Thus, the fight is half won by this predictability.

To win the other half, you simply must keep the distance stable, then 'shade' him with motion.

Figure out which way he intends, then lurch, and I mean in fractions of an inch, in a manner which will feed his intentions, then relurch in the other way. And this other way need not be in terms of inches.

Let me say it simpler.

If he moves away from you, you don't care.

He won't move sideways, because he is in attacker mode.

He will only move towards you.

As contact occurs, match his initial action. DO NOT RESIST!

When he blinks, reverse your action, and...abuse him.

Of course, if you use force, you have screwed up. (But if you have to, you have to.)

So try to use flow. Use a higher level, and learn how to protect him from his dangerous impulses.

Okay, even simpler.

If he punches, move back and guide the punch until he is off balance, then reverse your direction, and follow his punch back to him, and take advantage.

If he grabs, don't resist, go with him. He will quickly try to let go, but it is too late, and you can do what you want.

Okay, as simple as I can make it.
> If the force is greater flow it,
> if the flow is greater force it.

CHAPTER THIRTY-SEVEN
THE PHOENIX

Stand in a natural position. the feet should be shoulder width apart. The balance should be so that you can move in any of the eight directions of the compass easily.

Pivot to the left, the weight going onto the right leg. The left arm swings slightly out tot he side and the right arm comes up and is about to swing across the body.

Step to the left with the right foot, the weight going to the right foot. The right arm crosses the body and starts circling downward. The left arm comes upward in preparation for a strike.

Pivot to the right through an hourglass stance. The right arm swings down across the body as if blocking with the back wrist or setting up an upward scoop, and the left arm starts shooting across the body.

PIVOT TO THE RIGHT INTO A BACK STANCE WITH THE WEIGHT ON THE LEFT LEG. EXECUTE A RIGHT CROSS PALM BLOCK AND A LEFT SPEARHAND.

BEGIN STEPPING AROUND THE RIGHT FOOT WITH THE LEFT FOOT. AS YOU DO SO, BRING THE RIGHT ARM DOWNWARDS AND SWING THE RIGHT HAND THROUGH A CROSS PALM TOWARDS THE SUPPORT POSITION OF THE BUTTERFLY.

Finish stepping around the right foot with the left foot as you bring the right arm up to the butterfly position.
Walk the circle and do the form on the other side.
Then walk the circle back to do the next form.

BUTTERFLY PA KUA CHANG

PHOENIX APPLICATION

THE ATTACKER PREPARES TO PUNCH.

THE ATTACKER STEPS FORWARD WITH THE RIGHT LEG AND EXECUTES A RIGHT PUNCH. THE DEFENDER STEPS FORWARD AND SLIGHTLY OUT WITH THE LEFT LEFT AS HE EXECUTES A LEFT CROSS PALM BLOCK AND A RIGHT SPEAR HAND TO THE AXILLA (ARMPIT).

THERE ARE ABOUT A DOZEN THINGS YOU CAN DO AT THIS POINT, RIGHT OFF THE TOP. LET'S TRY A LITTLE MONKEY BOXING MATRIX KUNG FU, WHICH HAS ALL THE MONKEY BOXING TECHNIQUES IN IT.

The Defender wraps his right arm over the Attacker's right arm.

Moving the left leg behind the Attacker, the Defender keeps the Attacker's right arm trapped (and near breaking), and extends his left arm across the Attacker's throat.

The Defender steps all the way behind the Attacker's stance with a horse stance as he fully extends his intention across the Attacker's throat. the arm breaks, and the Attacker is dropped like a sack of stinky manure. Cool.

You will notice that you are actually using concepts from different Pa kua animals here. The entry is Phoenix, the arm wrap resembles the Snake, and the arm spread is Dragon. Good Pa Kua may mix the animals together, but you won't get there unless you separate all of the pieces of the animals in your mind first.

CHAPTER THIRTY-EIGHT
2BCBM

2BCBM means Two body Coordinated Body Motion.

From earlier courses you are no doubt familiar with the concept of Coordinated body Motion.

What this expands into, as you progress through the courses, is the ability to coordinate your body to his body, and thus take control of his body.

Hey, he has gone crazy and is trying to harm you, that means that he isn't controlling his body, and that means that you can.

He is giving it to you.

He is so mad that he is simply trying to give you his body.

Isn't that a nice way to look at a fellow so enraged that he is trying to end your odiferous existence on planet earth?

Now, 2BCBM can be learned simply through endlessly doing the techniques, but you should study the concepts, especially of distance and control, if you wish to achieve it in less than a lifetime.

The secrets are in these courses.

And, to be specific in this course, the secret is to do the instructions of this course...and master the concept of controlling distance.

2BCBM. It isn't even spoken of in hard arts, except in the most mysterious of ways. It's the Ki, you know?

Well, 2BCBM is not the ki, it's the key.

CHAPTER THIRTY-NINE
THE TIGER

Stand in a natural position. the feet should be shoulder width apart. The balance should be so that you can move in any of the eight directions of the compass easily.

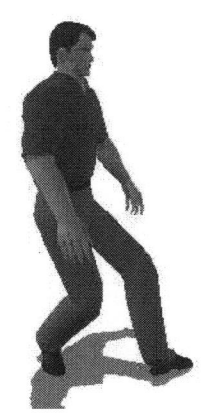

Pivot to the left, the weight going onto the right leg. The arms extended slightly outwards.

Step to the left with the right foot, the weight going to the right foot. The right arm crosses the body in an uppercut spear. The left arm is in a palm up position supporting the right elbow.

Pivot to the right to a back stance with the weight on the left leg as you execute a right high block and a left palm strike.

BUTTERFLY PA KUA CHANG

Begin stepping around the right foot with the left foot. As you do so, bring the right arm downwards and swing the right hand through a cross palm towards the support position of the butterfly.

Finish stepping around the right foot with the left foot as you bring the right arm up to the butterfly position and walk the circle.

THE TIGER APPLICATION

THE ATTACKER PREPARES TO PUNCH.

THE ATTACKER STEPS FORWARD WITH THE RIGHT FOOT AS HE EXECUTES A RIGHT PUNCH TO THE FACE. THE DEFENDER STEPS FORWARD AND TO THE RIGHT WITH THE RIGHT FOOT AS HE EXECUTES A RIGHT HIGH BLOCK AND A LEFT PALM TO THE CHEST.

BUTTERFLY PA KUA CHANG

The Defender steps forward with the left leg across the front of the Attacker. He maneuvers the Attacker's punch up as he executes a left elbow to the ribs.

The Defender spins to the right as he begins pulling down the Attacker's left arm.

The Defender steps back with the right foot between himself and the Attacker. He pulls the Attacker's arm down and executes an armbar.

CHAPTER FORTY
LOVE YOUR FELLOW MAN

Love your fellow man, and that means even the fellow who is trying to kill you.

Hey, he just doesn't get it, and he won't, if you don't give him a chance.

But 2BCBM, and all the benefits and abilities of the True Art, won't be yours unless you learn to love your fellow man.

Think about it this way.

Some fellow comes up to you and is enraged.

You can go away from him, or you can go towards him.

If you go towards him, the essence of a fight will occur (two terminals will collide).

If you go away from him, you are (thought of) as a coward. If you can get over other people's ideas of you, you just might save a life. (Although, to be honest, going away doesn't always resolve the situation).

The best thing to do is to maintain distance so that he can't touch you, and let him be angry and frustrated and so on until he gets over it.

Okay, think about it this way.

Some fellow comes up to you and is enraged.

If you get enraged also, then you have made his problem yours.

You have become him, when you should have maintained a stable emotion and let him become you.

In other words, if you respond in kind, then you have lost.

If you respond with compassion and understanding, then you both have won.

Okay, think about it this way.

Somebody tries to punch you, they are attempting to communicate with you. Best to handle the communication by accepting it, while not letting it actually come in contact with you.

And, doggone it, if he liked you enough to try to communicate with you, then isn't he your friend?
He just doesn't know it, yet.
But if you are gentle, and teach, and shed light, and share compassion, then maybe he will, and maybe you will have a life full of friends.

Think about it, and then do this:

DO THE ART UNTIL THE ART DOES YOU

CHAPTER FORTY-ONE
CREATING PA KUA CHANG

Art is the ongoing act of creation. Thus, learning the eight basic forms you have just learned is just the beginning.

To further create in Pa Kua you must learn to combine the eight forms. The way to do this is to do the first form, then, when you start to come out of it, do the second form. This must be done in a fashion that is smooth and flowing.

This is not difficult, it just requires a little thought, and possibly a little 'tweaking' of the motion.

Once you can do the first and the second form smoothly, do the first form and, when you turn out of it (go back to the circle walking) go into the third form.

Once that is accomplished, do the first form and the third form.

First and fourth. First and fifth. And so on.

Once you have completed this series of combinations, use the second form as your starting form, and figure out how to turn into the other forms one at a time.

Then use the third form as your base form, and so on.

1st Series of Forms.	Second Series of Forms.
Butterfly/Butterfly	Crane/Butterfly
Butterfly/Crane	Crane/Crane
Butterfly/Snake	Crane/Snake
Butterfly/Monkey	Crane/Monkey
Butterfly/Dragon	Crane/Dragon
Butterfly/Lion	Crane/Lion
Butterfly/Phoenix	Crane/Phoenix
Butterfly/Dragon	Crane/Dragon

Third series of forms.

Snake/Butterfly
Snake/Crane
Snake/Snake
Snake/Monkey
Snake/Dragon
Snake/Lion
Snake/Phoenix
Snake/Dragon

Fourth series of forms.

Monkey/Butterfly
Monkey/Crane
Monkey/Snake
Monkey/Monkey
Monkey/Dragon
Monkey/Lion
Monkey/Phoenix
Monkey/Dragon

Fifth series of forms.

Dragon/Butterfly
Dragon/Crane
Dragon/Snake
Dragon/Monkey
Dragon/Dragon
Dragon/Lion
Dragon/Phoenix
Dragon/Dragon

Sixth series of forms.

Lion/Butterfly
Lion/Crane
Lion/Snake
Lion/Monkey
Lion/Dragon
Lion/Lion
Lion/Phoenix
Lion/Dragon

Seventh series of forms.

Phoenix/Butterfly
Phoenix/Crane
Phoenix/Snake
Phoenix/Monkey
Phoenix/Dragon
Phoenix/Lion
Phoenix/Phoenix
Phoenix/Dragon

Eighth series of forms.

Dragon/Butterfly
Dragon/Crane
Dragon/Snake
Dragon/Monkey
Dragon/Dragon
Dragon/Lion
Dragon/Phoenix
Dragon/Dragon

Thus, there are sixty-four possible applications, just to start.

Matrixing a third form into this procedure will give you 512 potential forms, and the number of applications will become overwhelming.

And matrixing a fourth form will develop over 4000 forms.

And so on.

One should remember, however, the whole point here is not to have a static art that doesn't go anywhere, where the practitioner has to memorize endless techniques, but to create an artist who is able to analyze inside the moment, and to create, within the moment, a technique to fit the situation.

Thus, while one should try not to change the forms, one should be willing to tweak and adjust the forms when finding applications for them.

When one can change from form to form in Pa Kua ceaselessly and endlessly, and can derive a technique from any motion he creates, then he is there. He can honestly say that he is a martial artist.

EPILOGUE

As you proceed in your studies you will take note of a couple of things.

Pa Kua is quite heady stuff.

Pa Kua offers the chance to be truly creative.

But, while the flowery is fun, the function is what it is all about.

So, always concentrate on the basics, and make all moves functional.

This is the key to making sure that your Pa Kua doesn't degrade.

About the Author

Al Case walked into his first martial arts school in 1967. During the Gold Age of Martial Arts he studied such arts as Aikido, Wing Chun, Ton Toi Northern Shaolin, Fut Ga Southern Shaolin, Weapons, Tai Chi Chuan, Pa Kua Chang, and others.

In 1981 he began writing for the martial arts magazines, including Inside Karate, Inside Kung Fu, Black Belt, Masters and Styles, and more.

In 1991 he was asked to write his own column in Inside Karate.

Beginning in 2001 he completed the basic studies of Matrixing, a logic approach to the Martial Arts he had been working on for over 30 years.

2011 he was heavily immersed in creating Neutronics, the science behind the science of Matrixing.

Interested martial artists can avail themselves of his research into Matrixing and Neutronics at MonsterMartialArts.com.

Continue the Journey!

This book is the original manual that came with the video course of the same name. I will be putting the video half of this course on Amazon shortly. Search Amazon to find it.

There are several books on the Shaolin Butterfly and Butterfly Pa Kua Chang.

While there is value in all of them, there is a certain amount of repetition, so please be careful, examine the books carefully to make sure you aren't purchasing something you already have, or have no need for.

There is the 'Lite' Butterfly PKC, which is included in such books as 'Karate to Shaolin to Pa Kua Chang,' and in other places.

If you haven't done so already, you should examine the Shaolin Butterfly. In that book there is a method for the translation of shaolin into PKC, and for PKC into Shaolin. There is a lot more to be gleaned. I will be putting the Butterfly Pa Kua Chang on Amazon shortly, so do a search. If you can't find it you can always find it on my website, MonsterMartialArts.com,

If you are looking for other martial arts to compliment your education, on the next few pages you can find books and courses to aid you.

I specifically recommend Matrix Karate. Matrix Karate has the 'Matrix of Blocks,' which can be applied to the techniques you have seen in this volume, and which can expand your repertoire of usable techniques into hundreds of combat ready tricks.

If you are more interested in grappling, I recommend Matrix Kung Fu, which has the complete list of stand up takedowns.

THE 'HOW TO CREATE KENPO KARATE' SERIES!

How to Create Kenpo Karate
BOOK ONE
The Real History
Al Case

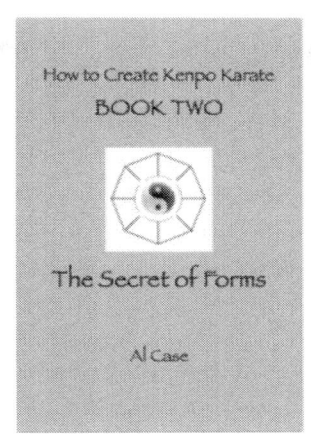

How to Create Kenpo Karate
BOOK TWO
The Secret of Forms
Al Case

How to Create Kenpo Karate
BOOK THREE
Creating a New Kenpo
Al Case

The most incredible analysis of Kenpo Karate in the world.
In depth Matrixing of over 150 Kenpo techniques.
New ways of doing Kenpo forms.
New ways of teaching and structuring classes.
A COMPLETE REWORK OF ONE OF THE MOST
IMPORTANT MARTIAL ARTS SYSTEMS IN THE WORLD!
Over 40,000 words
Nearly 400 pages
Over 800 graphics
Only possible through…

the logic of Matrixing!

The History of Matrixing

Matrixing is the cumulation of decades of research. Among the dozens of martial arts studied, Al Case kept specific records of five up to the point of Matrixing breakthroughs. The following five books are the encyclopedia of the history of matrixing.

These books are not arcane histories, but records of forms learned, techniques mastered, drills done, and so on. They provide, in addition, a linkage from Chinese martial arts through Karate to Matrix Karate, which was the first Matrixing course.

Pan Gai Noon (half hard/half soft) is a style of Chinese Kung Fu originally taught about 1900.

It was taught by a street hawker named Shu Shi Wa, and may have had roots in the Temple Gung Fu of the times.

It eventually was transformed into a style of Karate called Uechi Ryu.

The style therefore links Karate to Kung Fu, which makes it one of the more important martial arts, historically and technically speaking.

In this volume the art of Pan Gai Noon has been resurrected through the logic of Matrixing.

The first two forms, plus drills and techniques, are presented, making this a valuable addition to any martial artist's library.

Available on Amazon

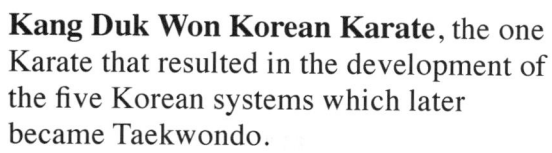

Kang Duk Won Korean Karate, the one Karate that resulted in the development of the five Korean systems which later became Taekwondo.

This is a pure form of Karate from before the Funakoshi and Japanese influence.

It was chosen by the Imperial bodyguards of three different nations, Okinawa, Korea, and Japan.

Available on Amazon

Kwon Bup is a form of American Karate developed by Sensei Robert Babich of the Kang Duk Won. It is linear and powerful, and the ultimate expression of the only American to ever do the 'One Finger Trick.'

Sensei Babich could thrust a finger through a board and not break it, but leave a hole. This is his art, his forms and techniques, his method of bringing Karate to the highest stage.

Available on Amazon

Outlaw Karate is the synthesis of two methods of Karate, Kang Duk Won (House for Espousing Virtue), and Kwon Bup (The Fist Method).

These arts were stripped of duplicate movements and poser techniques, then boiled down to six easy to learn (and thus easy to use) forms.

The result was a form of Karate that could be taught in less than one year, while keeping the original power of Karate, and even enhancing it.

This art set the stage for breakthroughs in the Martial Science of Matrixing. *Available on Amazon*

Any karate student wishing to learn an extremely powerful form of Karate, and to delve into the history of Matrixing, should definitely look into Outlaw Karate.

Available on Amazon

Buddha Crane Karate.
Matrixing is a form of logic.
While it can be used in any endeavor, it is specific to the Martial Arts.

Buddha Crane Karate is a very pivotal Martial Art as it was created just as the author was figuring out the logic of Matrixing.

In this book you get to see the exact thought process that is Matrixing at work; you will see the principles which would later crop up in his courses on Matrixing.

In addition, Buddha Crane is an entire Martial Art, built from the ground up. Thus you get to see exactly, how and why an art takes form. This will definitely enlighten any who wish to inspect their own martial art and truly understand what they are seeing.

Available on Amazon

Stand Alone Martial Arts Books

Following are stand alone books on a variety of martial arts. Matrixing has been used extensively to make these arts quicker, faster, and easier to understand.

Karate to Shaolin to Pa Kua Chang

The book that traces the evolution of internal power from Karate to Gung Fu.

There are three manuals in this volume, and they are designed to take the martial arts student from the hard knuckles of karate to the soft, internal practices of Gung Fu.

This book contains forms, techniques, training drills, and the theory necessary to help a student evolve quickly and natural.

Available on Amazon

Matrixing Tongbei

Introduces Tong Bei (through the back) Gung Fu. This includes basic theory and drills for creating a certain 'emptiness' inside the body.

Includes many matrixes for full and complete understanding of Tong Bei techniques.

This book is actually an introduction to the 'MonkeyBoxing' taught by Al Case. The complete line up of Monkey Boxing courses starts with this book, 'Matrixing Tong Bei,' and continues with the video instruction courses 'Blinding Steel,' and 'Matrixing Kung Fu (Monkey Boxing).

Available on Amazon

Fixing MCMAP: How to Make the Marine Corps Martial Arts into a True Martial Art

Military organizations the world over have long practiced martial arts, so the Marines decided they should have the best fighting art in the world. MCMAP is the result of intense research. A research conducted in the arena of real life and death struggles.

MCMAP is good. Really good, but there are some weaknesses in the system. There were certain limits on it, such as top level fighting was reserved only for men who advanced in rank. And, there were weaknesses such as no kicking structure, the system was designed with boxing as the template, weapons fighting was not taught as one, efficient subject, and so on.

FIXING MCMAP fixes these problems. So the person who studies these two volumes, Fixing MCMAP volume 1 and 2, will not only get the whole Marine Corps fighting system, but they will get the improved and fixed system. A system with no errors, and designed to make a true art, and which will make the BEST FIGHTING MEN IN THE WORLD!

Available on Amazon

Bruce Lee vs Classical Martial Arts

The most advanced book on Jeet Kune Do ever written. This book uses Matrixing, and even Neutronics, to finally and fully and completely understand The Little Dragon. Is Jeet Kune Do truly the best martial art in the world? When you apply Matrixing to it it may well be.

Yogata (The Yoga Kata)

The oldest exercise system in the world is at last put to a scientifically designed form. Easy to do, yet covers ALL the basics of Yoga. Good for warm up, cool down, or rehabilitating injuries.

This one form will enhance your martial arts, and your life, far beyond just doing the martial arts.

Black Belt Yoga

The art of Yoga arranged scientifically. Makes for MUCH faster progress in Yoga.

Instead of nibbling away at postures one at a time, the student discovers the totality of the method, and can see the end of the tunnel.

Why this hasn't been done before is actually one of the great mysteries of the world. It just makes SO-O-O much sense.

The Most Important Martial Arts Breakthrough in History

Matrix Karate

Five books detailing the entire system of Matrix Karate. This was the first course on Matrixing, and describes the procedure of matrixing. The system can be used as a template to matrix ANY other martial art.

The original book, on the original video course, was 160 pages. Thus, with over 650 pages, this series is an expanded viewpoint, answers more questions, gives more drills and techniques and exercises.

Matrix Karate, being scientifically designed, is not a style, it is a purity, and all other systems of Karate are substyles, or variations, of this one true Karate.

The Complete Series is available on Amazon.

The Universe of Al Case is Available at Amazon!

Discover unique worlds of imagination. Whole worlds of thought, unavailable to mankind, become known in these and other wondrous books. A more complete list of the works of Al Case may be found at:

AlCaseBooks.com

Printed in Great Britain
by Amazon